LEFT FIELD

LEGENDS

Mastering the Outfield

The Complete Guide to Left Field

Skills, Strategies, and Success

SKY BENSON

It is creative nonfiction, in this case. For various reasons, several parts have undergone variable degrees of fictionalization.

TABLE OF CONTENTS

CHAPTER 1

THE BASICS OF LEFT FIELD

Understanding your role

"And responsibilities."

As you take your place in left field on the big, green field, the sun shines on your glove. There is a lot of freedom and responsibility in this job, and you need to be able to combine athleticism, strategy, and mental attention in a special way. Let's look into the world of the left fielder and talk about the most important parts of being good at this important outfield position.

The Keeper of the Gap

Let's say a batter hits a screaming line drive into the empty space between centre field and left field. That's your area. Depending on how the team is positioned defensively, you are the main defender of this huge area, which includes everything hit from the foul line on the left side to straightaway centre field. It's an area that needs people with great range, or the ability to cover a lot of ground quickly and effectively. You have to get there in time to make the play, whether it's a hot liner or a high fly ball.

Getting Your Tools Sharp

Range is important, but it's not the only thing that matters. To make strong throws back to the infield when fielding ground balls, you need a sure glove and the ability to move quickly. Fly balls test your senses and how well you can follow them. You need to guess where the ball will land after it leaves the bat, run to where it will land, and call for the ball if it's close enough. Communication is very important here. If a fly ball looks like it's in centre field, yelling "I got it!" out loud can keep players from running into each other or dropping plays.

The Art of the Out

In left field, though, you don't just chase fly balls. There will also be times when helping out other outfielders is very important. In centre field, if a deep fly ball comes in, the player might need to move towards the wall. In this case, you become the second defender and are ready to catch the ball if it goes over the centre fielder's head. This takes good positioning in the outfield and anticipatory play, which means knowing where your teammates are playing and moving to match.

How to Think Like a Chess Master

Being athletic is important, but to play left field, you also need to have a smart mind. The hitter's position, the count, and the state of the game can all tell you a lot about the type of contact you can expect. It becomes second nature to know the park's dimensions, like where the wall is and how deep the outfield is in different spots. This helps you plan your move so that the best possible result happens.

This is the pressure cooker

Sometimes being in left field can make you feel alone. You might not get as many ground balls as players in the infield, but when you do, it can make all the difference. The crowd can go crazy when a player dives to catch a home run or grabs a line drive that's going to the gap. These plays can change the outcome of the game. As a left fielder, you need to be able to handle pressure. You have to stay focused the whole game, even when the ball isn't going your way, because it's all about making the play when the spotlight is on you.

The Unknown Hero

A lot of the time, left fielders don't get much attention, but their accomplishments are clear. They are the silent guards of the outfield, stopping hits that go over bases and possible runs. Being good at this role takes more than just athleticism. You need to be dedicated, focused, and know a lot about the game. The next time you play left field, know that you're not just watching over a patch of grass; you own the field and are ready to make every play count.

Advanced Strategies for Dominating from the Left Field

Now that you know what a left fielder's main duties are, let's look at some advanced strategies that can take your game from good to great.

As I read the hitter,

To learn left field, you have to stop being an observer and start making predictions. Pay close attention to the batter's position, the way they waggle their bat, and how they swing. All of these things can tell you a lot about their swing path and possible touch. You might hit a ground ball more often if your hitter has a closed stance and a short, tight swing. On the other hand, you might hit a fly ball more often if your hitter has a wide stance and a long, rolling swing. Look at what's going on in the game as well. Is there a runner on first with the sign to steal on? The batter might be more likely to try to hit the ball on the ground, which could lead to a double play. Knowing these subtleties will help you guess what kind of contact it will be and place yourself properly.

It's important to communicate

Even though being in left field can feel like being on an island, that doesn't mean you work alone. It's important to talk to your friends, especially the centre fielder. Talk about where you will be on defence for each inning depending on the batter and the situation. Use short, clear calls like "I got it!" or "You got it!" to keep players from running into each other and make sure that changes are smooth when fly balls are hit towards the gap. Never forget that a well-timed call can mean the difference between a catch that will go on TV and a frustrating ball that gets lost.

Getting Good at the Wall

The wall in left field can help you or hurt you. It is very important to know how big your field is and what kind of wall it has. It's either a padded wall that lets you do amazing jump-and-catch moves or a rock wall that makes you be more careful. During fielding practice, try hitting balls off the wall. Figure out how to judge the ball's carom and get ready for the second bounce. Making a catch off the wall that saves the game sends a strong message: you own your space, wall and all.

Awareness of the Situation

A good left fielder always knows what's going on in the field. Is there someone on second base? Knowing what's going on with the base runners can help you make decisions. For instance, if there is a runner on second and the ball is hit very far, you might choose to catch the ball for an out over trying to make an amazing diving catch that could cost you the chance and give the runner extra base. Being aware of your surroundings helps you decide what the best move is in any given scenario.

Giving your teammates a hand

As the left fielder, it's your job to protect your zone, but you also need to be able to work with others. Help the other outfielders catch deep fly balls. Be ready to cut off the centre player and make the catch if they need to if the ball is going towards the right-center gap. For this to work, there needs to be ongoing communication and planning. Being able to back up your friends without any problems shows that you are defensively aware and care about the team's success.

You'll go from being a good left fielder to a protective force on the field if you learn these advanced strategies. Remember that even though left field is a separate position, your success depends on how well your team does as a whole. Take on the task, work on your skills, and you'll become the left fielder that everyone counts on to make the play and secure the win.

Fielding ground balls

"And fly balls."

Left field is a big area of green that looks like it could be both a challenge and a chance. As the owner of this land, your success depends on two very important skills: being able to catch ground balls and find fly balls. Let's look at the techniques and plans that will turn you from a left field spectator into a defence powerhouse.

Mastery of Ground Ball

A hard hit ground ball screamed towards the gap can turn a calm afternoon at the ballpark into a fast-paced race. What makes a good grab different from an annoying bobble? To field ground balls, you need to have a low centre of gravity. Think of yourself as a spring that is wound up and ready to jump. You should bend your knees and keep your weight on the balls of your feet. This lets you respond faster and move your hand more efficiently to the throwing hand. A smooth ground-ball play starts with good footwork. When the ball gets close, shuffle your foot out to the glove side and step towards it. This lines up your body so you can move quickly and throw hard. Dive or spring for the ball, but keep your body still. This will help you keep better control of the game. When it comes to grounders, a solid glove is your best friend. Keep your glove open just a bit to make a pocket for the ball. Pay attention to where you catch the ball, not just where the tip of your glove is. This makes sure you have a good grip and lowers the chance of the ball popping out. It's important to be able to quickly switch from catching the ball to throwing it. Develop a quick, smooth motion in which you bring the glove close to your body, move the ball to your throwing hand, and step forward with the other leg at the same time. Do this transfer action over and over until it feels natural. Now comes the important part: the throw back to the infield. Strong throws that hit the mark can stop a runner at first or hit a baserunner who is trying to make a single into a double. To get power and accuracy, keep your elbow up and your throwing arm directed at the target. Pay attention to a smooth follow-through.

The Fly Ball Frenzy

Now let us look at the beautiful fly ball that flies through the air. To find fly balls, you need to be physically fit, focused, and have a bit of sense. "Eyes on the Prize" means to keep your eyes on the ball as soon as it leaves the bat. Don't pay attention to the batter or the people around you. Pay attention to where the ball goes, how it spins, and how it reacts to the wind. Prepare for its fall and move your position to match. For fly balls, the first burst of speed is very important. Do a quick crow hop as soon as the ball is hit. This is a small jump with one leg off the ground while the other leg lifts the throwing arm up and out of the way. You can quickly gain ground and get under the fly ball with this jump. Once you have some speed, look at where the ball is going and change your path accordingly. If it's going deep, quickly step back. If it's going shallow, quickly move forward. If the ball is close, don't be afraid to call for it. Just make sure you can hear your fellow outfielders so you don't run into each other. Put your hand under the ball as it falls and open your glove to make a pocket. You need to time your jump so that you catch the ball when it's at its largest. This makes it less likely that the ball will pop out and makes it easier to catch. Remember to use your glove to soften the blow so the ball doesn't pop out.

Making Practice Better

It takes time to get good at both ground balls and fly balls. Have a partner hit or throw ground balls at you from different directions. Work on your movement, moving the ball around, and throwing accurately. Hit fly balls in different directions with a fungo bat or a ball machine. Eye tracking, taking the best routes, and making catches are all things you should work on. Get better at second-bounce catches, carom, and hitting balls off the wall.

More Than the Basics

Technique is important, but don't forget how powerful attention and anticipation can be. Keep playing the whole time, even when the balls aren't coming at you. Check out the count and the men on base to get an idea of what kind of contact might be coming. You will change if you work at it and keep an open mind.from a player who reacts to a force in left field who acts.

Accept the Angles

Most of the time, ground balls don't move in straight lines. Learn to guess what angles they might take. If you hit the ball hard, it might take a wicked hop off the infield dirt, so be ready to change your playing position. If you know how different batters usually hit the ball, you can also guess where a ground ball will end up.

Why calling for the ball is important:

In the fields, communication is very important. If you're sure you can make the play, don't be afraid to call for a fly ball. A loud and clear "I got it!" can keep partners from bumping into each other and make sure the catch goes smoothly. But don't forget to make a choice. If you're not sure, tell your partner ("You got it!") so there is no confusion and no missed chances.

Getting Good at the Backpedal

To track down deep fly balls, you need to be able to backpedal. Keep your eyes on the ball and practise backpedalling easily. Hold your centre of gravity low and take slow, small steps. If you over-stride, you might lose your balance and find it hard to turn around fast.

How to Dive Like a Pro

There are times when a stunning diving catch is needed. Dive, though, shouldn't be your first pick. If you don't time it right, this move is dangerous and could hurt you if you don't do it right. If you want to dive catch the ball, make sure you give it your all and reach your hand out towards it. Always remember that player safety comes first.

How to Stay Focused

Sometimes being in left field can make you feel alone. When you don't do anything for a long time, you might get lazy. Set up a plan to help you stay focused during the game. To keep your body warm and your mind sharp between games, jog around the outfield or play shadow catch. Remember that your time could come at any time, so it's important to stay focused.

Getting better at games

Your "game sense" will get better as you play with more people. You'll start to guess what will happen based on the score, the batter, and the men on base. This gut feeling will help you place yourself better and make better choices on the pitch. Keep an eye on professional left fielders to see how they read the game and handle different conditions.

Implementing these suggestions and working hard at training will help you go from being a good left fielder to a strong defender. Left field is like a blank canvas—paint it with a beauty of great fielding!

Perfecting

"Your throwing mechanics."

The crack of the bat sends a rush of energy through left field. While running for first, your eyes are drawn to the ball that is hurtling towards you. In this single second, a perfectly made throw can change the outcome of the game. But a wild throw can cause chaos and could cost the team a run. This is where learning how to throw makes the difference between being a defensive liability and a game-changer in left field.

The Foundation: Making a Strong Base

A stable base is the first step to a strong and accurate throw. When you throw, a strong core is what makes you throw. During the throw, use your core muscles to keep you stable and give you strength. Planks, sit-ups, and Russian twists are all exercises that can help you get stronger in the middle. Your legs give you the starting speed you need for a strong throw. Squats, lunges, and plyometric jumps are good workouts to build leg strength.

A Step-by-Step Guide to the Throwing Sequence

For control and precision, you must have a firm grip on the ball. Outfielders often use the four-seam grip, but there are other types of throwing holds as well. Put your middle finger and index finger across the edges of the baseball, and then put your thumb on the bottom to hold it securely. Stand with your feet shoulder-width apart and your weight on the back leg. Bring your throwing hand back as you wind up, with the ball behind your head. The arm on the glove side should be bent a little in front of you. As you start to throw, take a strong step forward with the leg opposite your throwing hand. If you're right-handed, this would be your left leg. This gives you speed and helps you put your body weight into the throw. As your front foot falls, your throwing arm cocks back even more, putting stress on your shoulder and elbow. This is the point of greatest potential energy, which is like cocking a catapault. "The Unwinding" is where the magic takes place. Start to unwind your body and arm while your front foot stays on the ground and your core is tight. As the arm whips forward in a controlled circle, it lets go of the ball at its highest point. Do a full follow-through after throwing the ball after letting go of it. This helps keep the balance and makes sure the fastest speed.

Keys to Power and Accuracy

Having strong arms is important, but getting power through a smooth, controlled arm motion is even more important for accuracy. Think of whipping your arm like a slingshot instead of slam-dunk throwing the ball. Keeping your throwing elbow high throughout the move helps you use the right mechanics and keeps you from getting hurt. When you throw the ball, you might want to lead with your arm instead of your hand. It's important to have a balanced and efficient stride. Your front foot should land with a slight angle towards the goal. This will give you a stable base for the throw. As with any skill, getting better at throwing requires a lot of hard work. To improve your form and build muscle memory, do drills like wall throws, plyometric throws, and long toss.

Tips for Getting the Most Out of Your Performance

Before you catch the ball, think about where you need to throw it. This lets you plan your throw ahead of time, which helps you throw faster and more accurately. Use full-power throws not all the time. Learn how to change how you throw based on what's going on. It's sometimes better to throw quickly and accurately to first base to stop a runner than to throw hard to the plate. Professional outfielders often crow hop or wait a bit before throwing to trick baserunners and make them think about their lead. Try using different strategies to keep the runners on base wondering.

First Safety

Always put good mechanics ahead of brute force. Arm injuries can happen if you throw too hard or with bad form. Pay attention to your body, and as your strength and skills get better, slowly increase how hard you throw.

If you want to be a good left fielder, you should work on getting better at throwing. If you work on building a strong base, making your throwing motion smooth, and practicing regularly, you can go from being a liability on the field to a defensive tool for your team. A well-placed throw can change the course of the game, making you a true left-field legend.

CHAPTER 2

MASTERING THE WALL

Playing balls off the wall

"And making catches at the fence."

You can see left field. Not only is it a big area of green grass, but there is also a strong wall around it. This wall might help you or hurt you. A good left fielder can hit balls off the wall and make great plays at the fence, but a great left fielder can do both.

Getting to Know Your Wall

Walls come in many forms. Some are padded, which lets you do cool things like jump and grab at the last second. There are some that are brick, so be more careful. You should check out your wall before you try any deeds. You can be more daring when the wall is insulated, but you have to be more careful not to hurt yourself when the wall is made of bricks.

Getting Better at Practice

You should learn about the wall before the game. As part of your exercise routine, you should do wall drills often. The wall can be hit with fly balls by a partner. This will help you read the carom and make second-bounce stops better. Pay attention to your form when you jump against the wall, and let your body and hand take the impact.

Looking at the carom

You have to guess how the ball will bounce off the wall to do well with wall plays. The point at which the ball hits the wall, its speed, and the wall's material are all things that can change the rebound. As you play more, you'll learn where the ball goes after it hits the wall. Watching clips of professional left fielders making wall catches will help you figure out where they stand and how they plan their moves.

First Safety

It's fun to make a catch that would go on the highlight reel, but the safety of the players comes first. Don't try to catch something you're not sure about. Put your safety first and let the ball bounce back into the field if it is going in a dangerous way against a brick wall. When you play catch, remember that it's only fun if you're fit enough to do it.

Getting in touch is important

When you play balls off the wall, you often work with other people. The corner is where the right and left fields meet. If the ball is going there, talk to your right player. Make a lot of noise if you think you can catch the ball, but be ready to give up if your partner can see it better. When said at the right time, "You got it!" can keep the game from going wrong.

The Art of the Wall Grab

The blood flow speeds up as the ball moves faster towards the wall. Think about where you'll be when the ball hits and get ready for it. You might need to move back a little if the wall is padded so you have room to jump and catch. When the ball hits the wall,

"The Jump" means to jump quickly and hard. If you jump high, you can catch the ball when it's at its highest point. But don't lose your balance and don't jump too high or at an odd angle. The way you hold your hand should be open and facing the ball. For a safe catch, close your hand when the ball gets close. Don't forget to soften the hit with your hand so the ball doesn't fly out.

Plan B

Even when you're ready, the wall can surprise you. If you miss the catch, have a backup plan. Get ready to catch the second bounce and throw the ball hard back into the infield so that if you miss, the damage will be less.

Keeping Your Attention

Wall plays are fun to watch, but left field can get quiet at times. Keep your mind on the task at hand at all times. Be careful during the whole game. During breaks, you can watch Picture Wall and work on your jumps. This will help you remember things for when the wall comes on.

You have to work hard, practise and know your baseball park well to be able to hit balls off the wall and catch them at the fence. There are a lot of things that go into it, like knowing your boundaries, putting safety first, and getting along with your partner. You can switch from left field to strong defence and be able to catch and throw out any fly ball if you take on the wall.

Understanding the dimensions

"Of your home field."

Imagine yourself conducting a patrol in left field, with the sun shining off your glove as the crowd roars in excitement. Before you can properly claim ownership of this land, however, you must first have an understanding of its distinctive geography, which includes the proportions of your home field. Not only are these stats statistically significant, but they also serve as a map that directs your placement, your readings on fly balls, and ultimately, your effectiveness as a left fielder.

Unlocking the Secrets of Numbers

The majority of baseball fields are roughly constructed in the shape of a diamond, with foul lines going from home plate to the outfield boundaries. It is the most important piece of knowledge for a left fielder to know the distances between the outfield walls. It is essential to have a precise understanding of the distance between home plate and the left-field wall, the center-field wall, and the location in the outfield that is the deepest. These lengths decide whether a potential home run, a deep fly ball that you need to chase down, or a routine out is considered to be a home run. Certain areas of the outfield walls are deeper than others, which results in the creation of "power alleys" where home runs are more likely to occur. The ability to predict probable long balls and modify your positioning accordingly is made possible by having a solid understanding of these zones. Having a clear understanding of the precise limits of foul territory is essential. If the ball lands just a hair outside the foul line, it is considered a fair ball, and you will need to be ready to follow it down so that you can catch it. On the other hand, a fly ball that appears to be catchable but really lands just within the foul line is considered a dead ball, which subsequently results in an out.

This is how we transform numbers into knowledge

One stage is to be aware of the dimensions; but, in order to genuinely possess them, it is necessary to transform this information into knowledge that can be put into practice. Close your eyes and visualise the layout of your home field. This is the first step in the "Visualise the Field" exercise. Consider the outside walls of the outfield and the distances between them and home plate. Imagine a number of various scenarios, such as a line drive into the gap or a soaring fly ball towards the power alley. Walk through these scenarios in your imagination. You will be able to internalise the dimensions of the field with the help of this visualisation.In order to mimic the crucial distances on your home field, you should make use of field markers or cones during your practice sessions. In order to become comfortable with the area that you will be monitoring, you should practise using drills that replicate chasing down fly balls that have been hit to varying depths. It is a powerful instrument to have knowledge of the tendencies of the hitters your opponent employs. Is there a particular type of batter who is known for hitting bombs to left field? The anticipation will cause you to position yourself somewhat deeper. What is the name of a left-handed batter who is known for hitting line drives down the left-field line? Make the necessary adjustments to your positioning.

Putting Yourself in the Right Position

When it comes to placement throughout the game, the dimensions of your home pitch are a significant factor. If you are playing shallow fly balls, you should position yourself closer to the infield. This will help you to make a quicker throw to the plate in the event that a runner tags up on the fly. It is necessary for you to alter your position in accordance with the progression of the fly ball. If you are aware of the spot in the outfield that is the deepest, you will be able to determine the distance that the ball will go and position yourself to catch it before it hits the wall. Left fielders are frequently referred to as "gap patrollers" due to the fact that they are in charge of the huge area that is between the centre fielder and the foul line. Having knowledge of the dimensions will assist you in determining the optimal posture for you to cover this gap in an efficient manner.

Beyond the Numbers

There is no doubt that the dimensions of your home field are significant; however, they are not the only thing to consider. One of the most crucial factors that might influence the path that a fly ball takes is the wind conditions. It is possible for a normal fly ball to be transformed into a potential home run if there is a strong breeze blowing across left field. Pay attention to the direction in which the wind is blowing, and alter your positioning accordingly. As was mentioned previously, the material of the outfield wall can have an effect on the way a ball bounces along the wall. When playing near a brick wall, it may be necessary to take a more careful approach, whereas when playing against a padded wall, it is possible to play more aggressively. Don't let the numbers control you; instead, adjust your strategy to fit the given circumstances of the game. It is possible that you will play a fly ball somewhat shallower in order to prioritise a quick throw to the infield when there is a runner on second base and there is a possibility of a double play.

You can turn yourself from a passive observer to a proactive defender by being proficient in the dimensions of your home pitch. You are able to anticipate fly balls, make smart adjustments to your positioning, and finally, you are able to dominate your domain with self-assurance. The stats are simply a starting point; your commitment, practice, and intuitive understanding of the game will transform you into a force that is out of the ordinary and must be taken seriously.

Practicing wall drills

"And situational awareness."

Left field is a huge area in front of you, and you're going to put a masterpiece of defensive skill on it. But getting good at this area takes a lot of practice, working on both your physical and mental skills. This chapter will teach you about wall drills and situational awareness, which are two very important skills you need to improve from being a good left fielder to a defensive rock.

From Doing Wall Drills Over and Over to Mastering Them

The huge outfield wall can be both scary and exciting at the same time. Wall drills fill in this gap, making controlled practice into getting ready for heroics in real life. You will need a partner and a ball for this game. Have your partner stand about 10 to 15 feet away from a padded wall and throw fly balls at it from different directions. Work on judging the carom and making sure you catch the ball with a smooth glove transfer as you practice getting the ball after it bounces off the wall. This drill mixes tracking with working with the wall. While you backpedal and keep your eyes on the ball, have your buddy hit or throw fly balls at the wall. Time your jump to catch the ball as it bounces off the wall. This drill helps you get better at following deep fly balls and responding to the way they bounce off the wall. Explosives and wall awareness are both part of this drill. Put your back to the wall and stand close to it. When your partner throws a fly ball, do a crow hop, which is a short jump with one leg, and turn towards the wall. Catch the ball on its second bounce. You will be able to respond faster and make better catches near the wall after doing this drill. This drill makes things more difficult. Make your partner throw a bunch of fly balls at the wall all at once. You should work on getting a clean catch on the first ball and then finding any other balls that bounce off the wall. This drill makes you feel like you're under a lot of pressure from multiple fly balls in a game.

Outside the Wall

Don't forget that wall drills are only one part of the picture. Stand from the wall at different distances every time. You can practice different fly ball depths and wall interactions by moving around. Have your buddy throw fly balls at the wall from different angles to help you get better. This helps you get used to different caroms and bounces that can happen at any time. It's important to push yourself, but safety should come first. Do not try any risky jumps or catches close to a brick wall. As you do the drills, picture yourself catching the ball off the wall to win the game. This upbeat image can help you feel better about yourself and concentrate better.

Being aware of your surroundings: the mind of a left fielder

Sometimes being in left field can make you feel alone, but having a sharp mind is just as important as having a strong arm. Situational awareness, or being able to read the game and guess what will happen, is what sets great left fielders apart from average ones. The count, which shows how many balls and strikes were thrown to the hitter, can tell you a lot about the type of hit that is likely to happen. If the batter has a 3-0 count, they may be more likely to go for it, so you need to play deeper to prepare for them. Look at the batter's position, how they swing, and their past at-bats. Has he been known to hit fly balls or line drives? He either pulls the ball to left field or throws it all over the field. Knowing how the batter usually hits will help you guess the direction and type of contact. The number of base runners can have a big effect on where you stand. You might play a fly ball a little shorter for a faster throw to the infield when there is a runner on second base and a possible double play. Keep in touch with your friends all the time, especially the centre fielder. Talk about where you will be positioned for each inning based on the batter and the situation. An "I got it!" at the right time can keep players from bumping into each other and keep play smooth when fly balls are hit towards the gap.

Getting better at games

Knowing the rules isn't enough to be situationally aware; you need to build a sixth sense for the game. Pay attention to how professional left fielders stand in different scenarios. Find out how they read the batter, the men on base, and the flow of the game as a whole. Every game is a chance to learn something.

After each game, look at how you did and try to figure out where you could have positioned yourself better or been more aware of what was going on around you. Use what you've learned to make better choices in future games. Left field can be a quiet spot at times. Do not lose your attention for long periods of time. Think about what would happen in different situations, picture yourself making plays, and stay alert during the game. If you lose focus, you could lose a key out.

How Skill and Mind Work Together

Situational awareness makes you smarter and wall drills help you get better at using your body. Putting these two things together makes you a complete left fielder, ready to take on any task the game throws at you. As you walk onto the field, keep in mind that you're more than just a player in left field. You're also a strategic thinker, a master of anticipation, and a formidable defence force. You'll go from being a good left fielder to a defensive rock if you work hard at practice and are always hungry for more information. Your skill, focus, and unwavering desire will leave your mark on every game.

CHAPTER 3

OFFENSIVE

CONTRIBUTIONS

Hitting for power

"And consistency."

The sound of the bat hitting the ball. The noise of the crowd. A flying ball that goes over the fence and out of sight. These are the times when you really hit hard in baseball. But power that isn't stable is just a dream. We'll talk about how to hit for both power and steadiness, which will turn you from a shy contact hitter into a feared force at the plate.

Putting together a Strong Base

You can start hitting for power long before you even get to bat. To generate bat speed and reach your full power potential, you need a strong base. Your core is what makes your swing go. Planks, sit-ups, and Russian twists are all exercises that will strengthen your core. This will make you more stable and help you move power from your legs to your swing more efficiently. For making power, you need legs that are strong. By doing squats, lunges, and plyometric jumps, you can make your legs stronger and more quick. This will help you hit the ball farther and faster. Your body is a very important part of bat speed. To get the rotational strength you need for a strong swing, do workouts like medicine ball throws and weighted rotational core twists.

Efficiency Is More Important Than Brute Force in Swing Mechanics

To power hit, you need to do more than just swing hard. It's about making sure the physics work well so that the ball gets the most power. For bat control, you need a grip that is comfortable and stable. Try different ways of holding the bat until you find one that lets you feel it and use all of your power. The first step is to take a steady, athletic stance. Your knees should be slightly bent, your feet should be shoulder-width apart, and your weight should be spread out evenly. You start the "load" part when the pitcher is getting ready to throw. Your hands move back and your body weight moves back a little, making your swing twist like a spring. You start your step with your front leg when the pitcher lets go. This gives you speed and helps you turn your hips for power. The heart of your swing is your hips. When you take a step forward, quickly twist your hips, moving power from your legs to your arms. A smooth, controlled circle, not a rough hack, should be your swing. During the swing, keep your top hand on top of the bat, and after contact, fully extend your arms.

Consistency: How to Get Good at Making Contact

Power is fun, but a great player is one who hits the ball consistently. Pay attention to the strike zone. Don't chase pitches that are outside the strike zone. Be strict with yourself and only swing at pitches that you can regularly hit hard. Great hitters have great balance between their hands and eyes. Pay attention to when the bowler throws the ball and follow it all the way through its path. Bat control lets you change how you hit for different pitches. Don't just try for home runs when you practice hitting balls to all fields. Come up with a clear hitting theory. Do you hit for power and wait for the right pitch to hit the ball hard, or do you hit for gap and try to use the whole field? You will get better results if you know your skills and weaknesses.

Making Practice Better

Practice is the only way to get strong and reliable. Tee work lets you focus on certain skills. A stationary ball can help you work on your swing line, bat control, and timing. The front toss mimics live pitching but moves more slowly. So, you can work on your timing and focus on making good touch. The best test is live hitting practice against a pitcher. This lets you practice hitting balls that are thrown at you at different speeds and in different places, which helps you learn how to change your swing for each pitch.

The mental game is part of "Beyond the Mechanics."

Hitting isn't just about how your body moves; it's also a mental fight. Picture yourself hitting the ball hard and driving it with power. Visualising good things can help you feel better about yourself and concentrate better. Being tight can happen when you're under a lot of stress. Figure out ways to relax, like deep breathing, to stay calm at the plate. Every at-bat is a chance to learn something. After each at-bat, look at your swing and find ways to make it better. Don't think too much about a bad swing. Get over it, learn from it, and move on to the next pitch. It's impossible to win at baseball; even the best batters miss the ball.

Getting stronger and more consistent is a process, not a goal. It takes commitment, hard work, and a love for the game. Sometimes the ball won't go as far as you thought it would, which can be annoying. For those who are determined to keep getting better, you can go from being a hitter who is having trouble to one who is a force to be reckoned with. Power is fun, but being consistent is more important. With both skills under your belt, you'll be a full hitter who is always a threat at the plate. Now, go out there and hit like a power hitter! Make your mark on the game!

Smart base running

"And understanding situational baseball."

Base running, with its scary slides and stolen bases, is often seen as the flashier part of baseball. There is an art to "smart base running" that requires understanding the game and making smart choices that help your team score as many runs as possible. We'll talk about smart base running and situational baseball strategies here. These will help you go from being a careless base runner to a smart one on the base paths.

What you need to know about smart base running

For smart base running to work, you need to start with the basics. Getting a good lead off base lets you respond faster to a hit ball. If you want to steal bases or get into scoring position, this will help you get going. Pay close attention to how the pitcher throws the ball. Learn to spot their tells, like how they wind up differently for a fastball and a curve ball. This can help you guess what the pitch will be like and act accordingly. Learn the mechanics of running bases, such as the right way to slide, how to round bases quickly, and how to read your coaches' base running signs.

Thoughts Beyond the Base

Smart base running is more than just going from one base to the next. The count, which shows how many balls and strikes the hitter has received, can tell you a lot about how the pitcher is feeling. There is a good chance to steal a base when the batter is down 3-0. They might be more likely to swing for the fences. The number of outs and the score have a big effect on how to run the bases. The game is close, and there are two outs. A runner on first might not try to steal to avoid a double play. Look at where the outfielders are standing. How deep or how shallow are they playing? If you know this, you can choose when to tag up on a fly ball or take an extra base on a possible hit.

The Art of Making the Right Move in Baseball

When it comes to baseball, situational baseball is what holds smart base running together with the overall game plan. If there is a runner on first and a batter who is known for making contact, the coach might call a "hit and run." As soon as the pitcher starts to throw, the runner takes off, which forces the defence to throw quickly and could lead to a score. A sacrifice fly can be a smart move when there are men on base and less than two outs. The batter hits a fly ball far enough to score the runner after being tagged, moving the team forward without giving up an out. This is a dangerous move that could change the outcome of the game. The infielders move very close to the batter when there is a runner on third and less than two outs. If the batter hits a ground ball, the infielders are ready to make a quick double play, which could stop the runner from stealing home. Things change when you have two outs. It's risky to steal bases now that getting caught does not take long. Depending on the score and number of men on base, it can still be smart to take an extra base on a hit or force a throw.

It's important to communicate

Smart base running depends on being able to communicate well. Your teachers tell you how to run the bases by using signs. Quickly learn how to read these signs and act accordingly. Runners on different bases should talk to each other and share knowledge about the pitcher, where the fielders are, and possible next plays.

Getting more aware of your surroundings

Situational awareness is a skill that needs to be worked on in baseball, just like any other skill. Look at how professional base runners decide what to do in different game settings. Look at their plans and take what you can from them. Every game is a chance to learn something. After the game, think about how you could have made better base running decisions in different situations. Think like the coach does. What made them ask for a certain play? How might your running around the bases have changed the result of the situation?

From a careless runner to a strategic force

By learning the basics of smart base running, knowing how baseball works in different situations, and becoming more aware, you can go from being a careless runner to a strategic force on the base paths. When you're on the field, you act like the coach and make decisions that help your team and the offence as a whole. Smart base running isn't about flashy slides or home runs; it's about making smart choices that set up runs, make it possible to score, and put pressure on the other team. If you want to help your team win, even if it means giving up a personal stat, you have to look at the bigger picture.

Utilizing your speed

"And agility on the bases."

The sound of the bat hitting the ball. The noise of the crowd. You quickly nod and wave at the third base coach as you look at him. It's time to go. It's not enough to just steal bases as a fast and agile base runner. You need to use your natural skills to become a constant attacking threat. You can use your speed and agility to your advantage on the base paths by following these tips. You'll go from being a fast runner to a problem for the other team.

Building the Base: Training for Speed and Agility

Running to first base well requires a lot of raw speed and quickness. Do sprints as part of your workout programme. Watch out for bad form, like a forward lean, strong leg drive, and strong arm swing. To get used to what you'll be doing on the base tracks, practice both short bursts and longer sprints. Do hopping exercises, ladder drills, and cone drills as part of your agility training. You will need to be able to make sharp turns and dodge tags, so these drills will help you improve your footwork, coordination, and speed at changing directions.

Learning How to Run from the Bases

Without the right method, speed and agility don't mean anything. Getting a good lead off base lets you respond faster to a hit ball. You should get better at taking bold but controlled leads that don't go too far from the base. For a steal to go through or to get into score position, you need a strong first step. Focus on getting the most power out of your powerful starts while standing, and try to avoid wasting any movement. The right way to slide is to master the skill. Sliding well will help you avoid injuries and safely touch base. For stealing home, practice slides with your feet first and slides with your head first.

Making the Most of Your Speed

Now it's time to put what you've learned into practice and dominate the field. This is the best way to see how fast and alert you are. Learn how to read the pitcher, guess when they will throw, and get a perfect jump off of second base. Remember that you need to know more about the situation than just being fast to pull off a successful steal. Your speed can be used as a tool even if you don't steal. Take an extra base on a possible out to force the defence to throw, which puts pressure on the infield and opens up chances to score. If there is a runner on first and a batter who is known for making contact, the coach may tell you to "run on contact." This means running as soon as the ball is hit, which will force the defence to make quick plays and could lead to scoring chances.

Your secret weapon is speed

Being agile is more than just being able to run quickly in a straight line. To round bases quickly without losing speed, you need to make quick turns. To stay in control, practice sharp turns at full speed while keeping good form and shortening your steps. Base runners need to know how to avoid being tagged, especially when the play is close. It will be hard for the defence to tag you out if you practice making sharp cuts and being quick. A good base runner needs to be able to read the play and act quickly. Because you are so agile, you can quickly change your path, turn around, and respond to throws.

Getting better at base running

What makes great base runners different from good ones is their ability to turn their physical strengths into reflexes. You have to know the score, the number of outs, and the runners on base in order to make the right base running choices. You can figure out the risks and benefits of stealing bases, taking extra bases, or running on contact if you know what's going on. Pay attention to how the pitcher throws the ball. Look for a small pause, a different windup for a breaking ball, or anything else that might help you guess the throw and get a good jump. Stay in touch with your coaches and coworkers at all times. Learn how to run from the base and pay attention to what your teachers say.

Being mentally tough is like having a sharper sword.

The ability to move is only one part of the puzzle. Always be alert and pay attention. Don't let the crowd or the game situation take your attention away. Always keep your eye on the ball and be ready to act at any time. It will be close calls and times when you doubt. Get strong enough in the mind to get past your fears and trust your gut. Taking calculated chances is part of the game, and sometimes a brave base runner does well. Every time you run to first base, you learn something new. Go over your choices, both the ones that worked and the ones that didn't, after the game. This will help you get better at following your gut and make smarter choices in the future. Have faith in your skills. It's okay to trust your speed, your quickness, and your judgement. Being sure of yourself lets you play strongly and make plays that change the game.

This is Beyond Speed: The Complete Base Runner.

Being quick and flexible are helpful, but they're not the only things that make a good base runner. Figure out what's going on and make smart choices that help your team. It's important to know when to steal, when to take an extra base, and when to stay safe. Situational awareness means being aware of what's going on around you on the field. This shows where the fielders are, where the ball is, and what the score of the game is. What you do at base running will be better if you know more about the game. Learn about the different ways to run the bases and how they affect the game as a whole.

Letting Out Your Inner Speed Demon

Your natural speed and agility can make you a force to be reckoned with on the base paths if you train hard, improve your skill, and keep your mind sharp. You'll always be a danger, which will put stress on the defence and give your team chances to score. Your speed and agility are natural skills, but your hard work, intelligence, and love for the game are what will really make you a base running weapon. Your lightning-fast speed and natural brilliance will leave their mark on every game.

CHAPTER 4

Building Speed and Range

Drills and exercises

"To increase your speed."

The sound of the bat hitting the ball, the clamour of the crowd, and the thumping of your heart as you make your way back home. On the baseball field, speed is a highly prized asset because it enables players to steal bases, turn singles into doubles, and make plays that can completely change the course of the game. What are the steps you need to take in order to realise your full potential and become a true speed demon? For the purpose of enhancing your running speed and transforming you from an average runner into a blazing blur on the basepaths, we will provide you with a number of drills and exercises that are meant to help you achieve this goal.

Strength training and conditioning are the building blocks of the foundation.

It is not enough to only possess quick legs; one must also possess a sturdy and robust body in order to achieve speed. Squats are an excellent exercise for building explosive leg power, which is the basis for a powerful stride. As your strength increases, begin with squats using only your own bodyweight and progressively add weight. Lunges not only strengthen your legs but also enhance your balance and coordination, all of which are essential for running effectively. Put your attention on preserving correct form by keeping your back straight and ensuring that your knee does not extend beyond your toes. The deadlift is a powerful exercise that engages your entire posterior chain, including your hamstrings, glutes, and back, allowing you to move forward with greater force. Begin with a soft touch and concentrate on correct technique to prevent damage. How it works Exercises that feature explosive leaping motions are known as plyometric exercises. These workouts develop your muscles to generate maximal power in a short period of time. Box jumps, squat jumps, and depth jumps (advanced depth jumps) are some examples of exercises.

Drills for Speed Development

The term "strides" refers to brief intervals of rapid running that are typically between fifty and one hundred metres in length. Put your attention on sprinting with the correct technique, which includes a powerful arm swing, high knees, and a powerful leg drive. In between sets, take a minute or two to rest, and as you gain stronger, progressively increase both the distance and the intensity of your workouts. Hill sprints are a great way to push your leg muscles and generate explosive strength. Search for a hill that is not too steep and run as fast as you can to the top of it. In order to recuperate, you should walk or jog back down. Continue doing this for a number of sets. These drills are designed to help you build speed and acceleration from a standing position. Begin with rapid shuffles and work your way up to explosive beginnings with high knees and arm swings as you advance. Concentrate on reaching your maximum speed as rapidly as possible.

Don't Forget the Turns When You're Working on Your Agility

It is pointless to have speed without agility. Footwork drills such as ladder drills are great for improving your coordination and agility. Train your feet to perform a variety of footwork patterns while maintaining a light footing. Cones should be arranged in a sequence, and you should sprint around them while swiftly changing directions. Your ability to make accurate turns on the basepaths will be enhanced as a result of this. In this exercise, you will jog in a sideways motion while simultaneously kicking your legs out in front of and behind you. It enhances your hip mobility as well as your ability to move laterally. Before engaging in any sort of speed training, you should always undertake a dynamic warm-up in order to get your muscles ready and save yourself from damage. Try not to put too much pressure on yourself too soon. You should take recovery days and gradually increase the intensity and duration of your workouts. It is crucial to have proper running form in order to maximise your speed and prevent injuries. Training for speed does not have to be a burdensome process. Find a training partner to keep you motivated and incorporate exercises that you enjoy doing into your routine.

You will notice that your running form is becoming more efficient, that your strides are growing longer, and that your total speed is increasing if you dedicate yourself to these drills and routines. In a short amount of time, you will be a true menace on the base routes, leaving the defenders in the dust!

Reading the ball off the bat

"And taking efficient routes."

When you play baseball, you have to make quick choices. You have a very important job as a fielder: you have to react to the crack of the bat and catch the flying ball before it finds a hole. But how do you go from being a confused observer to being a magician who can tell where the ball will go? We'll talk about how to read the ball off the bat and take the best routes, which will turn you from a confused fielder into a defence master.

This is the science behind the art

It's not enough to just guess where the ball will go when it hits the bat; you also need to know how the swing works and how the ball moves. The ball's path is affected by its speed as it leaves the bat in a big way. It's possible that a faster ball will go farther and stay in the air longer than a slower one. The ball's flight path depends a lot on the angle at which it leaves the bat. The line drive will go fast and low, while the fly ball will go higher and farther. If you swing the bat faster, the ball may leave the bat faster and at a different angle. You can get a sense of where the ball might go by watching how the hitter swings.

As I read the hitter

As for the batter's hitting style, does he or she tend to pull the ball towards you (right-handed pull hitter) or throw it all over the field? Knowing how they usually hit will help you guess which way the ball will go. The count, which shows how many balls and strikes were thrown to the hitter, can help you figure out how they'll move. A batter with a 3-0 count might be going for broke, which could lead to a fly ball.

Tracking: The Art of Seeing It:

Look at the spot where the bat and ball touch. This lets you see right away what the launch angle is and where the ball is going at first. "Track the Ball" means that you should keep your eyes on the ball after you hit it. Keep your attention on its direction, taking into account wind conditions that could change it. Pay attention to how the other outfielders' hands move when you play with them. When the ball is hit deep, this can help you figure out its depth and direction.

Taking Quick Routes

You can move after you "read" the ball. Your first step needs to be powerful and move you towards where the ball is expected to go. Putting things off wastes important time. To hit a line drive or ground ball, you should move in a straight line towards the ball. If you don't have to, don't waste time going backwards or around in circles. For fly balls, you have to take a curved path, running backwards at first and then cutting towards the ball as it falls. The angle is based on how the fly ball was launched and how far it went.

Making Practice Better

Get better at keeping track of balls hit by a coach or partner. In a safe setting, this lets you improve your ability to focus.Either use a fly ball machine or have a partner hit fly balls for you to catch and track. This makes you feel like you're in a game and helps you get better at angled runs. Do drills that teach you how to read the hitter, follow the ball, and take the best passes. Work with your coaches and friends to make up situations that are like games.

After the Drills

Look at videos of great outfielders. Watch where they stand, how they take their first steps, and how they get to the ball. Look at how you did in each game and make changes as needed. You should think about times when you could have gone in a different direction or paid more attention. Keep in touch with the other outfielders at all times. Talk about positions before each inning and call out fly balls to keep players from running into each other.

You can go from being a passive watcher to a defensive force by learning how to read the ball off the bat and take the best routes. You'll be able to guess where the ball will go, respond very quickly, and make catches that amaze everyone. It's not about raw force; it's about reading well, moving quickly, and keeping your mind on the task at hand.
That's why keep training,

Covering ground

"And backing up other outfielders."

It can be both scary and exciting for fielders to see how big the outfield is. It is your domain, and you must take it over. But you need to do more than just catch fly balls to beat it. It's about quickly covering long distances, guessing what will happen next, and supporting your friends without any problems. Here's how to go from being an outfielder by yourself to being a master of space management and a trusted backup who makes sure the ball never gets past the green pasture.

Getting to Know Your Range:

Knowing your limits and making the most of your skills is the first thing you need to do to master the outfield. If your arm is strong, you can throw runners out at home plate or chase down base runners who are trying to turn singles into doubles. But don't think your arm is stronger than it is. Make sure you play deep enough so that you can easily make throws. Check how fast and agile you are. Can you run faster than anyone else on your team? This will help you figure out which direction (left, centre, or right) lets you get the most done. Regular practice sessions working on your throwing precision and covering ground will make your outfield range a lot better.

It's important to communicate

Talk with your fellow outfielders about where you will be before each inning. When choosing how deep to play, things like the batter's handedness and the direction of the wind should be taken into account. There should be no doubt that the outfielder who is closest to the ball should call out "fly ball" when it is hit. This keeps people from running into each other and lets everyone know who is in charge of the catch. If you have a good chance at a fly ball, don't be afraid to call for it. On the other hand, if another outfielder has a better view, let them know so there is no misunderstanding.

How to Get Good at Covering Ground

Your first step should be powerful and push you towards the path the ball is likely to take, especially if it's a line drive or a fly ball. When you need to cover ground for balls hit between you and another player, choose the route that goes straightest. To stop the ball, this could mean running diagonally or at an angle. You will need to cut off a ball hit to another outfielder sometimes, mostly when it's a hard-hit line drive or a deep fly ball. Talk to each other clearly and stop the ball at a safe distance to keep people from running into each other.

How to Back Up:

Think about where you think the ball will be hit and plan ahead. If someone on your team goes for a line drive, you should be behind them to catch the ball if they miss. When you're backing up your teammates, stay at a comfortable depth that lets you respond quickly and throw to the infield if you need to. It's not just catching missed fly balls when you back up. Be ready for things that you didn't see coming, like wild throws or balls that bounce off the wall in a strange way.

Getting better at things

Do drills that are meant to help you cover ground and back up your teammates. A lot of the time, these drills involve working with coaches or teammates to act out game conditions. Play games where you need to help a partner catch a deep fly ball. This means figuring out where the ball is going and getting ready to catch it if your partner misses. In these games, coaches or teammates will hit fly balls and line drives to different parts of the outfield. You'll have to respond quickly and cover a lot of ground while helping your team.

After the Drills

Look at videos of great outfielders. Watch where they are positioned, how they talk to each other, and how they cover ground and help their partners. Look over how you did in each game afterwards. Find times when you could have done a better job of placing or communicating. Get excited about what's going to happen on the field. To naturally know where to stand and how to best help your team, learn to read the move and the situation.

You can go from being a lone defender to an important part of the outfield machine by learning how to cover ground and back up your peers. As a true team player, you'll be ready for plays, cut off balls, and stop extra bases. You'll also be known for always being there for your fellow defenders. Even though the outfield is very big, if you work hard, talk to your teammates, and know your job well, you can turn it from a scary space into a fun place to play where you're in charge and make sure no ball gets out.

CHAPTER 5

THE MENTAL ASPECT OF LEFT FIELD

Staying engaged

"And focused during the game."

Be patient and pay attention when you play baseball. Along with physical skills, you need to be mentally tough. Long games, breaks in the action, and the constant chance of a long fly ball can make it hard to stay interested. Here are some tips to help you keep your mind sharp and focused on the game so that you're always ready to make a play when the time comes.

Getting Ready for the Game

Before the first ball, you can set yourself up to stay focused. A clear mind is one that has had enough rest. Get enough sleep before the game to make sure you're awake and sharp. Make a plan for before the game. This will help you get in the right frame of mind. This could mean doing routines that help you imagine things, light stretching, or listening to music that gets you pumped up. Set clear goals for your success, both as an individual and as a member of a team. Keeping these goals in mind will keep you interested and driven.

Keeping Your Mind on the Game

Don't sit still for long amounts of time. To keep your mind and blood moving, move your weight, wiggle your toes, or do some small stretches. Keep an eye on both the hitter and the pitcher's count. Knowing what's going on will help you guess the next pitch and respond more quickly. Don't take part in the play directly, but pay attention. Pay attention to the runners on base, the pitcher's technique, and where the fielders are standing. This helps your mind stay in the flow of the game. Mentally practice possible plays you might see when you're not directly involved. Picture yourself swimming to catch the ball, throwing a strike to the batter, or completing a perfect double play.

Keeping a positive attitude

We all make mistakes, so don't beat yourself up about them. Do not think too much about a dropped fly ball or a missed throw. Clear your mind, take a deep breath, and get ready for the next play. Speak out in support of your teammates. A good mood with high fives, cheers, and positive words can help everyone stay focused and inspired. Don't let anger or frustration get in the way of your work. Hold back your feelings and keep a calm attitude.

Keeping yourself hydrated

Stay hydrated because being dehydrated can make you tired and less able to think clearly. During the game, take regular sips of water.

Fun is what baseball is all about. Enjoy the rivalry, the friendship, and the thrill of the game. It's easy to stay focused when you're having fun. By using these tips, you can stay focused and interested in the game the whole time. You'll be an important player for your team because you'll always be ready to make the big play that wins the game. In baseball, being mentally tough is just as important as being physically strong. Leave everything on the field and stay sharp!

Handling pressure

"In big moments."

A lot of things can happen in baseball. One swing of the bat, one flying catch, or one throw that is just right can change the course of the game. But these times often come with pressure, a smothering feeling that can make it hard to make decisions and do well. How to handle stress in important situations so that you can go from being a nervous wreck to a clutch performer ready to step up and lead your team to win.

Getting to Know Pressure

When things are at stake, it's normal to feel pressured. It's how your body gets ready to do something. However, if it's not handled well, it can work against you. In important times, everyone feels pressure. Even pros with a lot of experience feel a rush of adrenaline. Don't see it as a problem; see it as a normal reaction that can be turned into good energy. Big times give you a chance to stand out, show off your skills, and make your mark on the game.

Putting together a routine before the game

Picture yourself doing well in the big moment. Imagine that you make the crucial catch, hit the game-winning home run, or strike out the hitter with all the bases loaded. Mentally run through the play and focus on the good ending. Tell yourself nice things over and over, like "I am calm," "I am focused," or "I trust my abilities." These mantras can help you feel better about yourself and deal with stress. Do techniques for relaxation like deep breathing or meditation before the game. There are methods that can help you calm down and get clear-headedness.

Being in the Present Moment:

It's easy to feel overwhelmed by things when the pressure builds. Don't think too much about what might happen if you fail. Pay attention to the exact thing you need to do, like hitting the ball, making the catch, or throwing a strike. "Trust Your Training" means that you believe in your training because you have worked hard to improve your skills. When things get tough, trust your experience and your gut. Calm your heart rate down and clear your mind by taking deep breaths. Before and during the play, take slow, deep breaths to stay calm and focused.

"Learn from Your Mistakes"

Even in the most important situations, everyone makes mistakes. If you make a mistake it, but don't think about it too much. Move on to the next play, shake it off, and come back better. Think about the times you did well under pressure in the past. Remind yourself of what you can do and use that to push yourself to do well in the moment.

Take advantage of the support system:

You can count on your friends to help and support you. Help each other out, talk to each other clearly, and remember that you're all in this together. Believe what your coach says and follow the game plan. They will help you do well and show you the way.

Getting used to pressure is a skill that you gain over time. If you work hard, prepare, and keep a positive attitude, you can change from a player who fails when things get tough to one who thrives in those situations. Take on the task and believe in your training. When the game is close, the best players step up to the plate.

Building resilience

"And bouncing back from mistakes."

Baseball is a beautiful game, but it also makes you feel small. There will be strikeouts, mistakes, and missed catches along the way. The real test of a player is not how well they avoid making mistakes, but how well they deal with them. Here's how to become mentally tough and learn from your mistakes so that you go from being a player who gives up easily to one who learns from their mistakes and comes back stronger.

Being okay with failing is part of the game

To get back on track, you must first realise that mistakes are a normal part of baseball. Some of the best players still miss catches and strike outs. "Reframe Your Thinking" means to stop seeing mistakes as failures and start seeing them as chances to learn. Every mistake you make is a chance to figure out what went wrong and get better. Problems and failures are chances to make your mind stronger. Accept that getting back on your feet will be hard and use that to fuel your drive.

What We Can Learn from Every Play

After making a mistake, think about what went wrong. It was a technology glitch, right? Getting off track? Figuring out what caused it helps you stop it from happening again. Don't be afraid to ask coaches or teammates for helpful comments. Their ideas can give you a fresh look at things and help you figure out what needs to be fixed.

How to Keep a Positive Attitude

Thinking about mistakes you made in the past is not helpful. Turn your attention to the present and the next play. Say positive things to yourself instead of bad things. Focus on what you can control and remind yourself of what you can do. Picture yourself pulling off the play the next time you're in a similar position. This upbeat thought can make you feel better about your self-worth.

Letting Go and Moving On

Learn to forget mistakes quickly. Don't let one bad play turn into a string of bad ones. Don't forget that you're part of a group. Your friends are there to help you and pick you up when you fall. Put your attention on helping the team succeed and forget about the past.

How to Make Your Mind Tough

Picture yourself regularly getting through tough situations and getting back on track after making a mistake. Mental exercises like these can help you get tougher. Don't worry too much about the results; instead, concentrate on how to play your best baseball. This helps you stay in charge and reduces your anger.

Learning from Other People

Watch how good players deal with mistakes. Find out how they stay upbeat and on task by looking at their habits and routines. Use the stories of players who faced big problems to become successful as examples. Their stories can really inspire people.

It's not easy to get back on track after making a mistake, but it's an important skill for any baseball player to have. If you take on the challenge, learn from every play, and keep a positive attitude, you can go from being a player who gets down easily when they make a mistake to a tough competitor who learns, adapts, and ultimately does well on the baseball field. The best players aren't marked by the mistakes they make, but by how well they can fix them and move on.

PREPARING FOR SUCCESS

Developing a pre-game routine

Being worried before a baseball game is normal. You can feel it in your stomach as the bat hits the ball and the crowd roars. But what makes a star performer different from the normal player? Most of the time, it's having a well-oiled pre-game routine. This personalised routine helps athletes make the most of their energy, clear their minds, and get their bodies ready to perform at their best. Here's how to make a pre-game routine that works for you and turns you from a nervous wreck to a focused player ready to take the field.

Knowing What You Need

Before a game, there is no one right way to do things. If you learn best by seeing things, adding visualisation activities to your daily routine can really help you. Think about making important plays, like hitting a home run or striking out the hitter. Kinesthetic learners learn best when they are moving around. A active warm-up, some light stretching, or even some grounders can help you get in the zone. Do songs or talks that inspire you help you concentrate? Using these sound cues as part of your practice can be very helpful.

Putting together your routine

Rest well. For peak efficiency, your body and mind need to be well rested. Make sure you have everything you need in your bag, and lay out your clothes ahead of time to avoid having to rush at the last minute. Allow plenty of time to get to the field and settle down. Do not rush, as this can make the nerves before the game worse. Light exercise, like jogging, jumping jacks, or light throwing, will get your heart rate up. It makes your muscles open and gets your body ready to move.

Tailoring Your Mental Get Ready

Set aside some time to do exercises that help you see things clearly. Picture yourself making good plays, being sure of yourself at the plate, or throwing the ball perfectly. This thought practice can give you a lot more confidence. Say good things to yourself instead of negative things. Believe in yourself and say things like "I am focused," "I am prepared," or "I trust my skills." If music or speeches get you going, make them a part of your routine. Do something that gets you ready to compete.

Connect with Team

Baseball is played with other people. Talk with your coach and coworkers briefly about your strategy and game plan. This brings everyone together and gets them ready for the fight that's coming up. Have some fun with your friends in a lighthearted way. Laughter, high fives, and good vibes can help calm people down before a game and make the environment more relaxed.

Last Touches

Be open and change your routine based on what you need and how the game is going. Try different things until you find what works best for you. Some players do better when they're alone, while others do better when they're with other people. Stick to your plan as much as possible once you find one that works. Being consistent helps you feel more at ease and less stressed before a game.

Creating a plan before a game is an ongoing process. You'll make changes to it as you gain knowledge to make it fit your changing needs. It's important to find a routine that helps you relax, concentrate, and get ready to do your best. If you do your pre-game process right, you won't be nervous when you walk out on the field. Instead, you'll be ready to make your mark on the game with confidence.

Scouting the opposition

"And understanding pitcher tendencies."

It is said that "knowledge is power," and in baseball, knowing your opponent is the best way to beat them. Here are some tips that will help you become a great scout and figure out how pitchers usually throw. This will give you a big advantage on the field.

Scouting reports are your secret weapon.

Scouting reports are very important in modern baseball. Does the hitter like to hit for contact or swing for the fences? Does he pull the ball a lot, or does he hit it all over the field? When you're in the field, knowing these patterns lets you guess where the ball might be hit. Does the other team have a history of stealing bases? How fast do they run to first? This knowledge helps the catcher and outfielders get ready for possible attempts to steal bases.

Watching the Game: Going Beyond the Reports

If you can, watch batting practice for the other team. Pay attention to how they stand, how they swing, and what kinds of pitches they hit well. While the game is going on, watch how the batters react to different pitches. Let me know if fastballs count as strikes. Do they hit breaking balls that are outside the zone? Look at their body language to get an idea of how they're going to talk to you.

Figuring Out the Pitcher's Tools

How well a pitcher does depends on how well they can keep hitters guessing. Watch how the pitcher throws to different batters at different times. Does his fastball come in handy early in the count? When he has two strikes, does he throw more breaking balls? Pay attention to where the pitcher throws his pitches. Does he favour the outside against people on the right? Does he test batters with fastballs that are too high? Finding these patterns can help you get closer to the zone and get better at recognising pitches.

Learn how the game works

Watch how skilled hitters deal with different types of pitchers. Look at how they hit and how well they do against different pitches. It's okay to ask questions. Don't be afraid to ask your coaches or teammates with more knowledge about how to scout pitchers and what they tend to do. Their ideas can be very helpful.

You can go from being a passive watcher to a strategic hitter or fielder by combining scouting reports with in-game observation and learning to figure out how pitchers usually act. You'll be able to predict pitches better, respond faster, and get a big advantage over your opponent, which will improve your chances of winning on the pitch. It is said that information is power. Be smart about it!

Nutrition, rest

"And recovery for optimal performance."

Baseball is a hard sport to play. During the game, you have to keep your mind and body at their best while swinging hard, sprinting quickly, and reacting quickly. Here are the best ways to eat, rest, and heal so that your body works like a well-oiled machine and you're ready to take the pitch by storm.

How to Eat to Succeed

Your diet is very important to your happiness. Make sure you eat a lot of fruits, veggies, whole grains, and lean protein. The nutrients in these foods are very important for your body to work well. Your body gets most of its energy from carbs. In order to keep your muscles fuel for games and workouts, eat foods like whole-wheat bread, brown rice, and pasta. Building and mending muscles need protein to work. A baseball player should eat a lot of lean protein sources, like chicken, fish, and veggies. Drink plenty of water all day. You should drink water most of the time. Try to drink a lot of water before, during, and after training and games.

A Time to Rest and Recover: The Silent Heroes

Aim for 7 to 9 hours of good sleep every night. Your body can heal muscles, get more energy, and think more clearly while you sleep. Light activities like yoga, walking, or swimming can help the body heal from hard games or workouts by increasing blood flow. Do not work out too hard. Learn how to tell when you're tired and take days off when you need them. Within 30 minutes of stopping a game or workout, eat a snack or meal high in carbs and protein to get your energy back.

Getting into the habit

Think about meal prepping to make sure you always have healthy, easy-to-make meals on hand. Set a regular sleep plan and stick to it, even on the weekends. Your coach can give you specific advice on what to eat and how to recover that is based on your exercise programme.

You can go from being a tired player to a well-rested athlete full of energy and ready to reach your full potential on the pitch by putting good eating, enough sleep, and effective recovery at the top of your list. When you take care of your body, you improve your performance, which lets you reach your peak and rule the baseball field.

CLOSING THOUGHTS

Baseball is a beautiful game that requires skill, mental toughness, and the ability to plan ahead. There will be ups and downs along the way, but the goal is always to get better. This e-book should have given you the information you need to make that trip go well. You can't learn all the skills you need to be a great baseball player quickly. It takes hard work and a commitment to always learning and improving your game. Do not stop learning and practicing the game. Most importantly, do not stop believing in yourself. When you get on the pitch, keep in mind what you've learned here: Read the ball off the bat, guess what the next play will be, and talk to your friends clearly. Accept the pressure, learn from your mistakes, and find a way to get in the zone before the game. Eat right, rest and healing should come first, and you should always try to be a good teammate. Baseball is a metaphor for life, not just a sport. You will face problems and hurdles, but if you are dedicated, persistent, and have a positive attitude, you can get past them and reach your goals in the end. Get your glove on and hit the field. Great players aren't born, they're made, one swing, catch or throw at a time. Have fun and good luck!